From the Heart of
The 10 Most Common Mistakes and How to Fix Them

An Experienced Editor and Qualified Proofreader Shows You How to Cut Your Copy Editing and Proofreading Bills

Sheila Glasbey

https://www.affordable-editing.com

Please note – this edition is for UK readers. Some of the things I mention are different in US English and probably in other variants of the language too. I hope to bring out a US edition soon.

Copyright © Sheila Glasbey, 2017

Cover illustration and internal illustrations © alexhallatt.com, 2017

Cover design by Indie-Go © 2017

Dr Sheila Glasbey has asserted her rights under the Copyright, Designs and Patents Act 1988 to be identified as the author of this work.

All rights reserved. No part of this publication may be reproduced, stored, or transmitted in any form, or by any means electronic, mechanical or photocopying, recording or otherwise, without the prior written permission of the copyright owner.

Introduction

You've spent months – possibly years – writing and revising your novel, short story compilation, poetry collection, technical handbook, dissertation or whatever, and making it as good as you possibly can. You've almost certainly had comments from friends, colleagues and fellow writers, and possibly paid for advice from a structural editor or critic. They have read your work and suggested changes, which you've painstakingly incorporated – or possibly rejected with contempt. You've re-read, re-hashed, revised, rewritten and re-everything-ed you can think of to polish your prose to perfection.

And now your book is ready to submit to an agent or a publisher, or perhaps to self-publish in one form or another.

But is it really, truly, ready to go? Your best friend with a degree in English found some typos. We all make plenty of those and it's very easy to miss them in your own work. Your mother found a few more. You discovered some further ones yourself and, rather worryingly, you find a few more every time you read it through.

You were hoping someone would reassure you about that apostrophe on page 96 – should it be there or not? What about the comma on page 19? Should you close those quotes before the full stop, or after it? Should 'mum' be capitalised? What about 'my mum'? What's the difference between a hyphen and a dash and what are the rules (if any) for when to start a new paragraph?

You want your book to be perfect when that agent or publisher picks it up. OK, there's always a chance they will see through the grammatical errors and recognise its sheer brilliance beneath that buzzing cloud of misplaced apostrophes, but then again, they may not. They may fling it aside with disappointment or even disgust. Similarly, if the person reading your book is someone who has just paid for it, you don't want them to stop reading halfway down page 4 – or, worse still, demand their money back – because they can't work out who's speaking.

I should declare myself here to be a professional copy editor – someone who is paid by others to check their work for grammatical errors, punctuation problems and low-level stylistic mistakes. I am also a qualified proofreader – someone who does the last-minute check that there are no typos in the manuscript prior to publication. People send me their writing before submitting to publishers and agents or publishing it for themselves. Back in the days when typesetting was a physical process, copy editing was done before the typesetting, and proofreading afterwards. These days, the term 'proofreading' is often used to cover both copy editing and proofreading, and the distinction has become less important, since most typesetting is now done electronically.

Anyway, however you describe the process, it's a time-consuming job and it doesn't pay particularly well, but some of us enjoy it (and are often labelled pernickety or pedantic by our friends, but we don't care because our real friends will put up with us anyway – we hope!).

One of the things I love most is picking up a book, potentially a brilliant book, whose surface appeal is dimmed by a coating of errors, and polishing it to perfection – or as near perfection as that particular book can ever reach. It's a great feeling, and the authors I work with generally seem to be very pleased with the results, though they don't always accept every proposed change. (I wouldn't necessarily expect them to. Some things are a matter of opinion, though others most definitely are not.)

But, as I said, it's time-consuming work and, although the hourly rate is not great, copy editing an 80,000-word novel is never going to come cheap. I'd still recommend professional copy editing, however, before venturing into print. It really is worth it, just as paying for a professionally designed cover is almost always worth it, too. Ships and ha'p'orths of tar come to mind. You've (almost certainly) put a lot of work into your book, so please don't scrimp and spoil it at the end.

So why am I writing a book to help you do your own copy editing, if I'm also telling you that you need a professional to do it properly for you? Well, here's the thing. You can save yourself a lot of money by getting certain things right before paying for copy editing and proofreading. When someone requests a quote from me, I always ask, as do most sensible editors, to see a sizeable sample of the book first. This shows me how much work I'll need to do, and I will quote them accordingly for the job. If there are tons of mistakes, it will obviously cost them more. If it's close to perfect… well, you get the idea. But please bear in mind that a writer's idea of close to perfect isn't necessarily the same as a copy editor's. I've already told you, we're a pernickety lot.

Anyway, the more of your own copy editing you can do before asking for a quote, the cheaper that quote will be and the more money you'll have left over for that super-duper book cover or your holiday in the Bahamas or your next meal or whatever.

What I've done is to compile a list of the ten most common errors I've encountered in the work I've copy edited over the years. I haven't done a statistical analysis, so I can't honestly claim that they are in exactly the right order of frequency, but who cares? The chances are, most writers' work will contain at least some of these mistakes. By reading this book you will learn how to put them right or, better still, not to make them in the first place. Your editing bills will be reduced, I'll be able to get out into the garden that much sooner, and we'll all be happy.

So, here goes.

1: Dialogue

You can skip this one, clearly, if your book doesn't contain any speech. But I've put it first because it's the place where writers trip up most often. It's not just the dialogue itself and how to present it, but the way it interacts with other things like punctuation – before the comma, after the comma and so on.

Here's how to get it right.

Speech quotes

"Hello," said John.

Or you can use single quotes:

'Hello,' said John.

It's really up to you whether you use single or double quotes for speech. Just make sure you are consistent. Publishers often have their own style guides and will want to change it, anyway. No one will reject your book because you've used single quotes instead of double or vice versa.

If ever you should need 'quotes within quotes', then you should change from single to double for the 'inner' quotes, or from double to single if that applies. Remember to make sure that, by the end of the sentence, you've closed all the quotes you opened. And remember that the comma, full stop, question mark or whatever goes *before* the closing quote, as shown in the examples above.

There's a nasty little exception to this 'before the closing quote' rule. Beware! Look at the sentence below.

John told Mariella that he would like a 'miniature pig'.

What's going on here? I closed the quote before typing the full stop, but nevertheless this is correct. The explanation is that the quotes around 'miniature pig' are not speech quotes. Quote marks are being used here for another purpose – sometimes known as 'scare quotes'. When used like this, the closing quote comes *before* the punctuation mark, which in this case is a full stop.

If you're in the UK, that is. If you're writing for publication in the USA, the rules are different. If you've read books published over there, you may have noticed the difference. In US English, a non-speech quote works like a speech quote – the full stop comes first, before you close the quotes. It's the source of a lot of confusion – much more so than taps and faucets, tyres and tires, if you ask me – among poor struggling writers trying to get their punctuation right. It's not fair to either side of the pond, but it's the way things are.

Hesitations and interruptions

If the speaker hesitates, show this with an ellipsis (three dots). If the dots are followed by a word, there should be a single space between the last dot and the word that follows.

'I don't know what to... do,' said John.

It's optional whether you put a space before the first dot, but whichever you do, be consistent about it.

'I don't know what to ... do,' said John.

'I don't know what to... do,' said John.

Both the above are correct. If the dots are followed by a closing quote, you can leave no gap between the final dot and the quote, as in:

'I don't know what to...' said John.

It's also acceptable to leave a gap between the last dot and the closing quote, i.e.

'I don't know what to... ' said John.

You may find that leaving a gap before the final quote causes Microsoft Word (or whatever word processing program you are using) to insert the final quote the wrong way round. This is a pain. Don't try to get around it by inserting a 'straight quote' instead, as this looks wrong. The easiest solution I've found is to type two quotes, one immediately after the other. If the first one is the wrong way round, the second one will be the right way round. All you have to do is delete the first one and, hey presto, problem solved.

That's what to do if the speaker hesitates. If the speaker is interrupted, by someone else's speech or the ceiling falling in or whatever, you show this with a dash (not a hyphen, a dash. See (3) for the difference between the dash and the hyphen. Let's stick to one thing at a time).

'I don't know what to – '

At this moment the ceiling fell in.

Another point to note. If you, as the writer, interrupt a character to tell the reader who is speaking, you have to be careful. E.g.

'I fixed the ceiling,' said John, 'and then to my horror the wall fell down.'

The whole of what John says is a single sentence here. What he actually says is *I fixed the ceiling and then to my horror the wall fell down.* It's just that you interrupted him to tell your readers who was speaking. That's perfectly fine. But note two things. After *John* there is a comma, to show he hasn't finished his sentence. Also, the *and* with which the second chunk of his sentence begins is lower case – because it's a not a new sentence for John.

Now compare:

'I fixed the ceiling,' said John. 'Can I go for lunch now?'

Here, our plucky hero utters two distinct sentences. What he says is *I fixed the ceiling. Can I go for lunch now?* Because of this, two things happen. Firstly, there is now a full stop (not a comma) after *John*, to show he's finished his first sentence. Secondly, the *can* at the beginning of his second sentence has a capital – because it starts a new sentence.

It's as easy as that. Takes a bit of practice if you're not familiar with it, but you'll soon have it sussed. And believe me, about 40% of my time as a copy editor is taken up with fixing this. Translate that into 40% of your money and you have a big incentive to master it before sending your work to a copy editor – myself or anyone else.

You can't sneeze a sentence

Before we leave the delights of punctuating dialogue, let me mention coughing and sneezing. There's a difference between 'he said' and 'he coughed'. Yes, of course there is, you say – speaking is not the same as coughing. Obvious or what? But this leads to something that writers sometimes get wrong. Compare the following:

'I'm tired,' John said. 'The dust is getting up my nose. Can I stop now?'

'I'm tired.' John coughed. 'The dust is getting up my nose. Can I stop now?'

Remember the 'spot the difference' competitions from your childhood, where you were given two pictures and you had to spot the differences… no? Well, you're probably younger than me. Anyway – what you have to do here is spot the difference(s) between the two sentences above.

Aha! Yes, the first has *said* and the second has *coughed*. But that, as my history teacher used to say, is not the answer I was looking for [evil cackle]. Oh no, you stupid little girl! Then she would throw the blackboard rubber at my head. Schools were tough places in those days. But back to our two sentences. Can you find another difference between them?

That's right – after *tired*, there's a comma in the first sentence and a full stop in the second. Now, can you tell me why? That little girl on the front row who's too busy doodling in her notebook to listen to me? Yes, you…

OK, seeing as I'm not really a teacher I'll be nice to you. The reason is that *John said* is something called a 'speech attribution', whereas *John coughed* is not. Coughing is an action, not a way of saying something. You can't really cough words, any more than you can walk words or run words or stroke words or anything else like that, unless you're using language in a very fanciful or metaphorical way that we won't go into here.

Speech attributions include not only *said* but words like *shouted*, *yelled*, *screamed*, *whispered* and, if you're Enid Blyton, *expostulated*. They are all ways of saying things. Washing your hands is not a way of saying something; neither is scratching your left ear. Not of literally saying something, anyway. So, the following is wrong:

* *'I'm tired,' John scratched his left ear.*[1]

while:

'I'm tired.' John scratched his left ear.

is perfect, if not exactly deathless prose.

Get all these things right and your dialogue will sparkle, no matter how boring the things your characters actually say.

I suggest you make yourself a cup of coffee now, as a reward for getting through all that. It's not difficult but it takes a while to explain (and read). Give yourself a short break, then come back and

---

[1] The asterisk is the linguist's way of indicating that a sentence is ungrammatical. I'll use it in this book to mark anything, including spelling, that is wrong.

feast on the delights of paragraphs. The next section is shorter, I promise.

2: Paragraphs

When should you start a new paragraph? Well, it's kind of up to you, but sometimes it isn't. That's very clear, isn't it? No? OK, let me show you how.

The thing is, sensible paragraphing can help your reader to follow your story – or your cogent, well-reasoned argument or your persuasive piece of advertising, come to that – and that's what you want, isn't it? Happy readers keep reading and come back for more.

The rule you possibly learned at school was 'Start a new paragraph when the topic changes' – and that rule remains a good one in most contexts. However, there are other reasons to start a new paragraph, too. One important one in fiction is 'When the speaker and/or actor changes'. By actor, I don't necessarily mean David Tennant or Olivia Colman, though they would fit the bill as well as anyone else. I just mean the person doing or saying something or other in your story.

Let's go back to John and Mariella. John has finished his home improvements, I'm happy to say, and he and Mariella have escaped from their collapsing property and are sipping cocktails on the balcony of a Spanish villa overlooking the sea. Well, why not? The sun is shining as I type, and I can't help wishing I was there too.

'It's so lovely out here.' Mariella took a long drink of her delicious ice-cold strawberry daiquiri. 'Let's stay here forever and never go back to our place in Birmingham. The roof's probably fallen in by now anyway.' She gave a little wink to show John that she didn't quite mean it, though a bit of her would have liked nothing better than to stay there permanently.

John took a sip of his drink and gazed at the cloudless blue sky. 'I wish you had a bit more faith in my DIY skills,' he said sadly. Then he grinned. 'Though to be honest I'd love to stay here too.' He kicked the table leg in frustration. 'So unfair that I'll have to work for another nineteen years before retirement, and even when I do...'

Notice that I started a new paragraph when Mariella had stopped speaking, thinking, drinking, etc, and our attention turned to John. Then all his 'stuff' went into one paragraph too. It's a neat way of signalling when the focus changes from one person to another. Of course, a paragraph may consist of just a single sentence of dialogue or action – or even just a single word.

'Shall we stay here forever?' said Mariella.

'No.'

Mariella frowned.

'Just think about it.'

Notice that putting *Just think about it* on a new line signals to the reader that this is John speaking, not Mariella. This takes away the need to add *said John* in this case, which is neater, cleaner, and could save you two valuable words if you are hoping to reduce your word count for a short story competition.

Consistently adopting this paragraphing convention really is a great help to readers and can make your writing style more elegant and spare. Think of the clean lines of a modern bathroom. Now stop thinking about bathrooms and let's get back to our unfortunate couple, who shortly have to return to their collapsing Birmingham flat – one that I suspect may have an ageing bathroom, possibly with a nasty seventies-style coloured suite.

I should point out that in this book I'm separating my paragraphs by a vertical space, which is one way it can be done. Another way is to have no extra vertical separation between paragraphs, but to indent the first word of the new paragraph by several horizontal spaces. In novels, the second method is normally used. In other forms of writing, e.g. on a website, the vertical space method is more common. What matters most is to be consistent. Microsoft Word, or whatever word processing program you are using, allows you to set such things for the whole document. Make sure you learn how to do this, as it will ensure consistency for you.

But the main message here is *Give John and Mariella their own paragraphs* – not because it will save their marriage (though it might – we all need our own space), but to give your reader an easy time and keep him or her onside.

One final thing. If John or Mariella or someone else takes centre stage for a long time, without giving anyone else the chance to speak or move or take a sip of their drink or run away… you may find yourself without a paragraph break for several pages, and this is definitely *not* a good thing. If it happens, you could revise your text so that poor Mariella is allowed to get a word in, or even just scratch her left knee from time to time. Alternatively, you could start a new paragraph while John is still speaking and sipping and groaning and kicking table legs and all the other stuff he does. That's OK. You're allowed to start a new paragraph while we are still focused on John. Just make sure that when Mariella finally manages to break in to the narrative, she gets that new paragraph she so much deserves.

3: Punctuation

We addressed this to some extent in (1), but there's more. There's the question of lists and where to put the commas in them. There's the matter of when to start a new sentence. There are dashes and hyphens. I recently read a book produced by a reputable traditional publisher where they got this wrong. Yep. They used horrible little hyphens when they should have used long, cool dashes. Ugh. See, you can do better than some traditionally published writers, if you follow my advice here. Get one up on that snooty bunch, hah! Sorry, traditionally published people. No offence, honest. I've been one in my time.

Lists

OK, let's start with lists, as they seem to be everyone's favourite thing these days, on social media at least. I'm really talking here about lists contained within a single sentence, such as:

Mariella went to the market and bought apples, oranges, bananas, pineapples and cheese.

She and John are home from their Spanish holiday, by the way. The flat is still standing, for the time being at least. Marital relations are not good, but let's hope all that fruit will at least keep them regular.

This really is easy-peasy stuff. There's a comma after each item in the list, except the next-to-last one, *pineapples*, which has an *and* after it instead. That's all. You probably knew this already and are mildly insulted that I should even mention it. Sorry. But I wanted to lead in to the next thing, which is to say that this is a place where US English, as written by our American cousins, is different. They frequently use a comma before the *and*, giving:

Mariella went to the market and bought apples, oranges, bananas, pineapples, and cheese.

I have no idea why they do things differently over there – or why we do things differently over here, which is an equally valid way of looking at it. I should add, however, that there is a tradition in the UK known as the Oxford comma, which means that the extra comma, the one before the *and*, is used. (It's called the Oxford comma because it was traditionally used by Oxford University Press. I'm told that Americans call it the Harvard comma, which is interesting.)

Anyway, if you are writing for a UK audience and you use the Oxford comma, you may find yourself having to work very hard to defend yourself, though you will have the occasional vocal and articulate linguist on your side, so you may be in with a chance.

My advice, if you're writing for a UK audience, publisher, etc, is to keep things simple and avoid the Oxford comma, except on those occasions where the items in the list are long and unwieldy and you really need that comma to make sense of things. I'll let you make up your own example to illustrate this. I'm tired and hungry and ready to take a break. And I can see an articulate linguist approaching, so I'm off!

Hyphens and dashes

What's the difference and when should each be used? A hyphen is a short horizontal line used to join two words or to break a long word over two lines. An example of a hyphen is the one in *twentieth-century.* A further example is *twelve-year-old* – notice that there are two hyphens here.

Hyphens are inserted automatically by your word processing program whenever a word is too long to fit on the line. Because it's automatic, you don't have to worry too much about this, although there are ways to take control if you wish.

There is also a thing called a 'hanging hyphen', used when saying something like *Mariella likes nineteenth- and twentieth-century art.* See what happened there? Instead of saying *nineteenth-century*, the writer abbreviated this to *nineteenth*, but the hyphen was retained to make clear that *nineteenth* was intended to be attached to *century* in the reader's mind. These hanging hyphens are easy to forget. Get them right and you'll be every copy editor and proofreader's dream client, I promise you.

Which word combinations need hyphens, which ones have just a space between words, and which words are you allowed to join to make a single word with no space or hyphen? The answer here is not clear cut and, in many cases, there are no strict rules. Often, what seems to happen is that a new word combination is forged (*tool-bar, hyper-link* and once, long ago, *pigeon-hole*) and for a while everyone uses the hyphen to make this strange new word look a little more friendly and accessible.

As time goes on, we all become familiar with pigeonholes and toolbars or whatever, and the two words tend to merge to make a single word with no hyphen and no space. But there's often a longish period where any one of these options remains acceptable. That's why there are sometimes no right answers, though individual writers, and indeed publishers, may have very strong ideas on which variant should be used. Some copy editors can be very sniffy about it, too.

My chief advice is 'be consistent'. If you use *toolbar* in one place, don't switch to *toolbar* or *tool bar* in another. As an editor, I often find myself doing global searches of the whole book to check for these things, and it's surprising how many variants of a single compound word the writer has managed to use. Check your own work for this and, once again, you'll be ahead of the game.

While we're on the subject of global searches, remember to check the names of your characters for variant spellings too (Mary Ann, Mary-Ann, Mary-Anne, Marianne...). And check the colour of their eyes while you're at it – please!

Now for the dash, which, as I've already said, is longer and has an entirely different function. A dash is a sort of 'Hold off, wait for it, here comes the deal' signal to the reader. Let me use one to demonstrate – here goes. And another one – see what I'm doing here? If you look back at what you've read so far, you'll notice I've used a fair number of dashes – I like them. Some writers like them more than others. One of the reasons I like them is that I think they help the reader catch the intonation – the stress, the emphasis on certain words – that the writer has in mind. (Notice that in this last sentence I used a pair of dashes to contain a kind of example or elaboration of what I was talking about. This is another common use of the dash, but in this case make sure that you close your opening dash with another one.)

You'll find that that most keyboards only give you a little hyphen-sized horizontal line and not a dash, which is kind of annoying until you realise how it works. Actually, I still find it annoying, but there you go. There's something that looks like a longer dash, but that turns out to be an underscore, which is of very limited use in fiction. These_are_underscores.

So how do you type a dash? In Microsoft Word, if you type a single word and then the little dash and then another word, without leaving any spaces, you'll get *pig-iron* (or whatever). Fine, if a hyphen is what you want. But if you want to write *John has a pet pig – its name is Pedro*, then you need a dash. If you have certain options ticked in AutoCorrect, you can probably type a double hyphen (one hyphen followed by another with no space) and Word will convert it to a dash for you. If this does not work and you don't like delving into AutoCorrect and similar, you can do the following.

If you type *pig* and leave a space after it, and then type a hyphen followed by another space, followed by another word with a space after it – you'll find that, by the time you've done all this, your hyphen has magically turned into a dash, just as you wanted it to. (Occasionally I find that, in order to get the required magical transformation, I have to type a word I don't really need after the hyphen and then delete it once the magic dash has appeared. But hey, magic never comes cheap.)

If you're unfamiliar with this sleight of hand, try it. Practise. It really is much simpler than it sounds – though why they make us jump through these hoops is beyond my understanding. One of these days, I'll type a hyphen and a space, and a pair of white doves will fly out of my screen.

While we're on the subject, the minus sign is a different thing altogether, though it looks remarkably like a dash. If you are typing mathematical stuff, you'll need to go to the 'symbols' list, at least if you're using Word, and select the minus sign from there.

If you've studied copy editing or proofreading, or have read a treatise on these subjects, you may have heard of en-dashes and em-dashes. I haven't used that terminology here, as it's not really necessary. Use the short line for a hyphen and the long line that appears 'by magic' for a dash, and you won't go far wrong.

One final thing. Sometimes in print you'll see an extra-long dash between words, with no space on either side of it. This is a convention used by some publishers, though I think it's a little dated now. I would not advise trying to emulate it on a computer. There's probably a way to do it but it's almost certainly a big faff, and I'm really trying to keep your life simple here.

Here endeth the section on hyphens and dashes, you'll be pleased to know.

Commas

These far-from-timorous wee beasties can truly make a writer's (and a reader's) life a misery if you don't show them who's boss. Here's how to take control. We will also discuss the comma's rather stuffy and possibly a little poncey cousin, the semi-colon.

You may remember your English teacher telling you that a comma marks a pause. Well, that's often true, insofar as it goes. It can also divide a list into its elements, as we've already seen. You can use it to add a little something extra to a sentence, as I'm showing here, by putting a comma on either side of the extra bit. I'm sure you are familiar with all that. The trouble is, there's a fair bit of flexibility in many cases over whether or not you need a comma. Sometimes it's a matter of taste. Some writers would not have put a comma after 'The trouble is' in my sentence just above. I don't think it really matters in this case. (Or I don't think it really matters, in this case.)

There are times, though, when a copy editor is going to add commas or remove them, and you will feel they are doing it just to annoy you. Mostly, they aren't. Or mostly they aren't. Sometimes a well-placed comma can remove an ambiguity (an alternative meaning you hadn't intended. There are examples of these all over social media, some of them extremely rude). Or a comma can simply break things up a bit and make the reader's life a little easier, which of course is what you want. Or which, of course, is what you want. I really must stop doing this.

Here's an example of where it really matters. Compare these two sentences:

(a) The pig, which had a black mark on its face, was chasing John.

(b) The pig which had a black mark on its face was chasing John.

See the difference in meaning? Sentence (a) tells us, as a bit of extra information, that the pig that was chasing John had a black mark on its face. It supplies more detail. Sentence (b), however, helps us identify which pig we're talking about, as in *It was the pig with the black mark on its face which was chasing John.* Notice that the *which* in sentence (b) can be replaced by *that*, whereas the one in sentence (a) can't.

These sentence types are given fancy names by linguists, but the important thing for us is to get the commas right. Commas around the 'extra information' in sentence (a). No commas in sentence (b).

That's all. Again, if you get this right, you'll be coasting home. And please, please, ignore anything that the Microsoft Word grammar checker (and probably other grammar checkers too) may have to say on this subject. I want to shout rude words here, but I won't.

Distinguishing between the places where commas are really needed (or really *not* needed) and cases where it's a matter of choice or style is not always straightforward. Comma placement is both an art and a craft. No two writers (or copy editors) will ever completely agree. Aim for balance – not too many, not too few. Also aim for balance, in that if you use a comma to introduce a bit of extra stuff, remember to close it with another comma.

Leanne, the woman who sold John his pet pig was a farmer.

Add the missing comma here before making your coffee or whatever and taking another well-earned break.

The run-on sentence

You may hear these called all sorts of things, especially by harassed copy editors, but what they really are is sentences separated by commas when, as we all know, sentences should be separated by full stops. It's not the length of the sentence that's necessarily a problem – it's the way they are divided up. Let's have an example.

Mariella does not like John's pet pig, she told him he had to choose between her and it.

The problem here is not that this sentence is too long – it really isn't. It's possible to write much longer sentences that are absolutely fine. But here, the way the information is presented means that this really needs to be two sentences, separated by a full stop. A dash or a semi-colon would also be acceptable. The following are all OK:

Mariella does not like John's pet pig. She told him he had to choose between her and it.

Mariella does not like John's pet pig – she told him he had to choose between her and it.

Mariella does not like John's pet pig; she told him he had to choose between her and it.

Personally, I much prefer the full stop option in this case, but that is more a matter of style. These are all acceptable, whereas the comma option I showed you first is not.

Why? Well, I don't really have a deep explanation and I'm not convinced anyone does. I could go into linguistic contortions and start talking about clauses, independent or otherwise, but I don't think it's worth it. If in doubt, start a new sentence. This also has the advantage of breaking up your writing a little – ringing the changes. For the reader, a series of long sentences can be tiresome and dull, in any kind of writing. A few short ones break up the rhythm and wake your reader up, which can't be a bad thing. Can it?

Semi-colons

Semi-colons are OK but should be used sparingly. They are a little more acceptable in academic prose, for example, but in a novel you should aim to get by mainly with commas, dashes and, of course, the good old full stop. Having said that, the occasional semi-colon can be poignant and powerful. Be on the lookout for examples in your reading. If you find a good one, try to decide why it works so well.

4: Names, Roles and Capitalisation

In other words – mum or Mum? Now that's important, as your mum (yes, that's right) will tell you. Modes of address like 'sir' and 'madam' come into this too.

This section will be relatively short. I know I've said that before, but I really mean it this time.

Consider the following:

'Hello, Mum,' said Mariella. 'I've just been talking to Devonia's dad and he's offered to take the pig off our hands. I hope John will agree.'

Yes, it's our beleaguered couple again. Notice here that *Mum* has an initial capital, while *dad* does not. Now, who'd like to tell me why?

Yes, it's because *Mum* is being used here as a name – like *Mariella* or *Devonia* or *John* or any other name – while *dad* conveys a 'role' – as in *my dad, my father, my pig, my laptop, my editor, all mums, every dad I've ever met* and so on.

That's really all it is. We are used to writing *my mother* and *my father*, and probably would not dream of using an initial capital in these cases. But the phrases *my mum* and *my dad* for some reason often cause problems, probably because they are informal and occur less frequently in print. Aunts, uncles, nieces, nephews and all other relations work in exactly the same way, though they may not always offer to take extraneous pigs off your hands.

'Hello, Uncle Fred,' said John. 'Could I please ask your advice on keeping pigs? Mariella says they eat anything at all, but my nephew says I have to buy special food.'

Sir and madam

Now let's move on to 'Sir' and similar titles and modes of address. If I'm writing about Sir Anthony Arbuthnot or Lady Clarissa Chalkwood, then the *Sir* and the *Lady* need to be capitalised, as I've done here – because these titles are part of their names. It's just like *Mr*, *Mrs* and *Miss*, but with a bit more class (or affectation, depending on how you view these things). But if you're an ordinary guy and I'm addressing you, out of politeness, as 'sir', then this is not part of your name and needs to be in lower case. Ditto 'madam' (not 'madame', by the way. That's French).

Hello sir, hello madam. May I introduce you to my pet pig?

There you are – a lovely short section. I could say more but I won't. Feel free to play on social media for a while or, better still, take a little exercise.

5: Brackets (Parentheses) and Punctuation

Many of us call these things ( ) brackets, though they are strictly known as parentheses. Brackets can be square [ ] (in which case they are known, amazingly, as square brackets), or other fancy shapes like { }. Not that this really matters. What matters is that you place them correctly, and it can be trickier than you think. Nasty little beasties, parentheses... out to trick you, as is so much of English grammar, and probably the grammar of other languages too.

Actually, no, it's the commas' and full stops' fault. It usually is. Please observe sentence (a) below.

(a) Mariella sat at her desk, her head in her hands. They had now had the pig for three weeks (or four weeks, if you counted the trial period).

Look at the full stop right at the end. Note that it comes after the closing parenthesis. This is correct. Now compare (b):

(b) Mariella sat at her desk, her head in her hands. They had now had the pig for three weeks. (It was four weeks, if you counted the trial period.)

Let's play Spot the Difference again. You'll observe that, in (a), the bit in parentheses is not a new sentence – it's a continuation of the previous one. There's no full stop after the first *weeks* and no capital letter on *or*. Also, as I said above, the full stop right at the end comes *after* the closing parenthesis.

In (b), however, there's a full stop after the first *weeks*, and the stuff after the opening parenthesis is a full sentence in its own right. And this time the full stop right at the end is placed *inside* the closing parenthesis. (This works exactly the same if you have more than one sentence inside the brackets. It applies to other punctuation too, such as a question mark. See?)

Why all of the above? A good question. Again, it's hard to say exactly why it is the case. Perhaps it's best to think of it as a convention, rather than a rule that makes any logical sense (a lot of English grammar is like this). Best just to remember that, if you have one or more complete sentences inside parentheses, the full stop goes *inside* too. If, however, the stuff inside the parentheses is not a complete sentence but a continuation of the sentence before it, then the final punctuation mark, whatever it is, goes *outside* the closing parenthesis.

Whew. I hope I don't have to type the word *parenthesis* again for a very long time.

6: Spelling

'Oh, I rely on my spell checker for that,' I hear you say. Huh. Unless your spell checker is considerably better than any I've come across, you're on to a loser there. Spell checkers can help, but they're not enough and you have to use them with great care. The spell checker on my phone converted *Wow!* to *Qwerty!* the other day in a text I was trying to send. Why? Your guess is as good as mine. Is *qwerty* even a word, apart from being the first six letters on the third row down on my keyboard, and originally the first six letters on a typewriter? And no, please don't tell me that *qwerty* means something rude or unpleasant in urban slang – I really don't want to know, and where has my phone been to pick up language like that anyway? Hmm.

Be especially careful of words you think you know how to spell. We all have blind spots when it comes to spelling. *Misspelled* is one of them, amusingly. So easy to give it a single *s* and get **mispelled*. My spell checker got that one right, but if a spell checker flags up a mistake to me I always check with a dictionary. (If you use an online dictionary make sure it's a UK dictionary you are using – if that's what you need. Also, some spell checkers annoyingly change themselves to US spelling when you are not looking, and there are one or two words they unfailingly get wrong.)

If your characters enjoy creamy Italian cheese, or you write cookbooks, you may find yourself using the word *mascarpone*, which is another word a lot of people misspell. No, it's not **marscapone* – truly it's not. Look it up if you don't believe me.

Remember, too, that a bicycle has *pedals* and not *peddles*, and when you cycle uphill you are *pedalling* furiously against the gradient, not *peddling*, which means something different altogether, like trying to sell your ramshackle old bike by wheeling it from door to door to see if anyone will give you twenty quid for it.

A final example that many people get wrong – the words *palate*, *palette* and *pallet*. Three words, three spellings, three different meanings. Which is which? Your *palate* is the roof of your mouth. If you're an artist, your *palette* is the board where you mix your paints. Finally, a *pallet* is a straw mattress, a makeshift bed or a flat structure used for transporting goods. See Wikipedia or other sources for lots more information about pallets, which I certainly didn't know before checking the definition online just now.

Bear in mind that even the cleverest of spell checking programs can't really be expected to know which of these words you meant, so if in doubt, or even if you're pretty sure you know, look it up to make certain.

Something else it's useful to know to spell – the magic code for your discount on my services at https://www.affordable-editing.com/ is TheFourteenthPig. Don't ask me why – it's as close to random as my imagination can come up with. If you quote it in the email or form message you send to contact me, you'll receive a discount the first time you use my proofreading and copy editing services.

(For future work, you'll receive a discount for being a previous customer.) Of course, you may choose to share this code with the world, her husband and his pig, but may I respectfully ask that you don't? It would be good to be able to reward people for reading this book! Thank you.

7: Plurals, Possessives and the Greengrocer's (or Greengrocers') Apostrophe

The name of this is not really fair to greengrocers. Some of them are highly literate. There is quite possibly a greengrocer out there somewhere who has won the Man Booker prize. And, of course, other types of shopkeepers, and indeed non-shopkeepers, may fall foul of this little beastie too.

Problems with apostrophes are less common than you might think these days, which is why we're down at number seven here. The problem has been well publicised on social media and most writers get it right, though everyone makes the occasional mistake. Sadly, the focus on apostrophes has earned some of us poor devoted pernickety types the label of 'grammar police' or even 'grammar fascists', which really is unfair. Most of us are nice and some of us are very liberal in outlook. Some of us may even have voted Remain.

But let's not get into politics. Instead let's pay our troubled family, John and Mariella and their pig, another visit.

John and Mariella own a pig. Just one pig, not two pigs or three pigs or six pigs.

OK, so *pigs* is the plural of *pig*, with not an apostrophe in sight. That's how it should be.

Now let's give the pig a present, so that it becomes the proud possessor of a blue bow.

The pig's bow is a rather fetching shade of blue.

The pig now has not only a bow but an apostrophe too. The clue is in the word 'possessor'. The pig possesses a bow, and the apostrophe is used to indicate possession. A linguist would call *the pig's bow* a 'possessive'. It all hangs together.

If John were to acquire another pig and give that one a blue bow too, then we could say:

The pigs' bows are a rather fetching shade of blue.

The apostrophe now comes after the *s*, at the end of the word, to indicate that more than one pig is involved (I can just see Mariella's face).

As well as possessives, apostrophes can be used for the kind of abbreviation where you miss out a letter or two. We often say something like *I'm going to feed the pig* instead of the more tortuous *I am going to feed the pig*. The letter *a* has been lost from *am* and the two words have joined up to form the single word *I'm*, with an apostrophe in it to show that a letter has gone missing.

When you join up *she is* or *John is* in this way you get *she's* and *John's* respectively. These look a bit like possessives, like the possessive in *John's pig*, but they aren't. They just happen to look the same. This doesn't have any drastic consequences, because they all need apostrophes before the *s* anyway. The trouble starts when people (some people – not you, I'm sure) become convinced that every time a word ends with an *s*, you need an apostrophe before it. They end up inserting an apostrophe in a word like *apples*, where the *s* is simply meant to indicate that there is more than one apple.

The following sentence is b-a-a-a-d, very b-a-a-a-a-d. (Notice another use of the hyphen here, to indicate drawled pronunciation.)

*The pig's ate all the freshly baked pie's that John had slaved over all afternoon.

You can see where the term greengrocer's apostrophe (or sometimes grocer's apostrophe) came from. It can also justifiably be called the greengrocers' apostrophe, if you think of it as being associated with more than one greengrocer.

Its seems to be the word where most of these mistakes are made. Ask yourself, whenever you use it – could this word be replaced by *it is*? If the answer is yes, then use an apostrophe. If the answer is no, then don't.

This pig is a nuisance. It's eating all our food.

This is correct, because you could equally well say *It is eating all our food.*

Now consider:

This pig is a nuisance. I keep treading in its droppings.

Yep, this one's OK too, because you can't say **I keep treading in it is droppings.* The *its* here is a possessive, if you think about it, because the droppings belonged to the pig, at least before it dropped them, and you shouldn't add an apostrophe.

Who's afraid of the big bad apostrophe?

Before we finish with apostrophes, I should mention *who's* and *whose*. Again, this pair have had a lot of attention on social media and I can't help feeling there are some people who deliberately get them wrong, just to be annoying. No? Well, here's how to get them right.

John has a wife who's not keen on pigs.

This is correct, because the apostrophe tells us that a letter is missing. The full version, equally correct, would be:

John has a wife who is not keen on pigs.

The word *whose* is a different beastie altogether. Like *its*, *my* and *your*, it conveys possession.

John, whose wife Mariella is not keen on pigs, has a difficult decision to make.

Notice that you cannot replace *whose* here with *who is*. The result – no apostrophe.

Another example of *whose* would be in a question like:

Whose pig left that mess on the sofa?

Once again, you can't replace *whose* with *who is*, so there is no apostrophe.

8: Who Said That?

Ever played 'count the speaker'? A delightful game, guaranteed to brighten up your reading of the dullest book. It happens where the author doesn't bother to tell you who said what, sometimes for pages on end. You suddenly realise you don't have a clue who's speaking and, assuming you can summon up the will to go on reading, you turn back to the last recorded speech attribution (*said John*) and mentally supply the *Johns* and *Mariellas* up to where you'd got to. Or you count, and if it's even, it's John speaking – or should that be Mariella? – and if it's odd, you fling your e-reader out of bed or rip several pages from your glossy new paperback. And scream.

The answer is: Don't do it! Tell your reader who is speaking, at least every few sentences. A couple of times on each page is a good guide, but remember, pages on an e-reader can be quite short. And if John and Mariella are joined by Stuart or Devonia, you'll have to be even more careful, because you can't rely on pronouns (*he* and *she*) to distinguish among members of that group anymore.

Judicious paragraphing can also help in the speaker identification process – see (2) above.

9: Emphasis, *Emphasis* or EMPHASIS? (Please Don't Shout at Me!)

If you want to add emphasis to a word or phrase in your text, the usual way, in print, is to use italic font, *like this*. Bold font, **like this**, is useful for section headings and the like. Capitals should be used VERY SPARINGLY, and in dialogue are used to indicate SHOUTING. So, unless your character really is shouting, avoid them. Many text-to-speech programs interpret capitals as shouting, which may make life uncomfortable for your listeners. No one likes having their ears blasted, least of all our friend John.

'Get that pig OUT of my living room.' Mariella's eyes were blazing.

Here, Mariella is definitely shouting at her husband, and possibly at the poor pig too. By contrast, if *out* had been in lower case italics, we would understand that she was simply giving the word some extra emphasis. If you are already using italics for some other reason, you can always remove the italics or add bold to make the word stand out.

'Get that pig out *of my living room.' Mariella's voice, though soft, held a hint of menace.*

*'Get that pig **out** of my living room.' Mariella's voice, though soft, held a hint of menace.*

That's all, really. Easy to get right but it can make a big difference.

10: Mr and Mrs

No, not the TV game show, if you are old enough to remember it, which I most definitely am not. In UK English, *Mr* and *Mrs* are not followed by a dot, stop or period, whatever you want to call it – unless it's the end of a sentence, of course.

That's all. It's different in US English, where the said stop (or period) is, at least sometimes, used after both of these.

11: *Then* and Other Adverbs

I know, I know... I said there were ten. Sorry. But I just wanted to remind you that *then* is an adverb – partly because it's a favourite word of mine, but also in case you're a follower of the Stephen King[2] (and others) 'Ditch the Adverbs' school of writing.

Adverbs can be useful, that's all I'm saying. Don't overdo your use of them (she said fervently), but don't be afraid to use one when it's needed. Even Stephen King has been known to use a *then*. Use adverbs sparingly [adverb] and well [also an adverb].

---

[2] I do like his books. Just in case he's reading this (but I really do).

Final Tip – From One Who *Knows*...

Never, ever, ever, in your whole long life, do a global replace. Not for all the tea in China, as my mother used to say. Not for all the chocolate in Cadbury's. (Other makes of chocolate are available, especially Galaxy Salted Caramel – yum.) If you absolutely *have* to do a global search-and-replace, do the one where you check each individual change as you go, and make sure it's really what you want to do before you do it.

Consider what happens if you do a global replace of *Ann* with *Anne*, but neglect to select the 'whole word' option or the 'case sensitive' option or both. (Even if you do remember to select these options, it's possible to slip up if you don't check them one by one. Believe me, I know.)

There are a lot of words with the letters *ann* in the middle of them. In a whole novel, there are an awful lot. Good luck trying to reverse your global replace... because there are also many words with *anne* in the middle that you won't want to change. Global changes should be banned (or bannd?).

It's a nightmare. Be careful.

Finally finally – I wish you lots of luck, as well as lots of fun. Yes, copy editing can actually be fun. You too could become a pernickety pedant, just like me.

A Note from the Author

As I said earlier, if you get all the things in this book correct, or even most of them correct, you'll be way ahead of most writers. However, you would still be advised to have your worked checked by a professional copy editor and proofreader. I haven't covered absolutely everything here, and a few mistakes will inevitably slip in, however knowledgeable and careful you are. But you should find that, by paying heed to these points, your bill for copy editing and proofreading will be considerably reduced. It certainly will be if you employ my services, which you can find at:

https://www.affordable-editing.com/

If you mention, when you contact me, that you've read this book, and quote the Magic Code in Section (6), I'll make sure that you get an extra price reduction, over and above any other offer that may be ongoing.

If you've found this short book helpful, I'd also be very grateful for any comments or suggestions for improvement. Please contact me by email at:

roscov100@yahoo.co.uk

or via my Facebook editing page at:

https://www.facebook.com/affordable.editing/

or on Twitter at @Ros_Warren. (See below if the name change is puzzling you!)

My services include copy editing, proofreading and also higher-level 'structural' editing. In addition, I do ghostwriting and supply critiques and general advice on novel writing, submissions and publishing.

I write and publish my own novels under the pen-name Rosalie Warren. I have also had a number of books traditionally published. You can see my novels on my author website at:

http://www.rosalie-warren.co.uk/

Acknowledgments

My lovely cover image and the running pig within the text were created by Alex Hallatt. You can see Alex's website at:

http://alexhallatt.com/

The cover was designed by Indie-Go, who also did the beautiful cover for my novel Lena's Nest. I would strongly recommend their services.

http://www.indie-go.co.uk/services/design/

My website was designed by Melissa Lawrence, who also helped with publicity, background research and general encouragement. Her website is at:

http://www.melissalawrence.co.uk/

My appreciative thanks to everyone who has helped me with this book. Special thanks to Melissa Lawrence, Jan Needle and Paul Johnson for helpful comments and support. Several other colleagues at Authors Electric gave me useful advice, including in particular Chris Longmuir, whose excellent book Nuts and Bolts of Self-Publishing (2017) I would strongly recommend.

Finally, thanks to Paul for being there always.

Polite Request

Authors depend on word-of-mouth to sell their books, and because of this we very much appreciate reviews. If you have found this book helpful, please leave a review on Amazon or wherever you bought the book, or on the **Affordable Editing Facebook page** here: https://www.facebook.com/affordable.editing/

Thank you!

Printed in Great
Britain
by Amazon